SKI FEVER

SKI FEVER

how to master the fastest-growing winter sport

by Curtis Casewit

A Rutledge Book

HAWTHORN BOOKS, INC., PUBLISHERS
NEW YORK AND LONDON

Published by Hawthorn Books, Inc.

All inquiries should be addressed to Hawthorn Books, Inc., 70 Fifth Avenue, New York City 10011

Simultaneously published in Canada by Prentice-Hall of Canada Ltd., 520 Ellesmere Road, Scarborough, Ontario

Library of Congress Catalog Card Number 65-23629

Printed in the United States of America

First Printing

The author is indebted to many people for advice, suggestions: Willy Schaeffler, coach and teacher; Ed Hunter, for use of facilities of Winter Park, Colorado; Richard Oestrike, ski buyer and salesman; Gloria Chadwick, Pat Swenson of the U.S. Ski Association.

Cover: Monkmeyer Press Photo Service; photo by Perren. Pages 2-3: Sun Valley News Bureau. Frontispiece: Aspen Association. Contents page: David Stemple.

CONTENTS

Learning to ski at an early age gives confidence, strengthens muscles.

Chapter One

WHY SKI?

Against the whiteness of the snow, colors are livelier; skiers lounge on benches, sunning themselves. Under the blue sky, the skis make black, red, mauve, brown and white slashes against the racks; the bottoms of the skis are bright yellow, a startling green—even tulip red. Parkas have gay patterns; multi-colored pants are taut and smart. Faces shine. Somehow, everyone is handsome here. The sum of all this beauty makes the heart beat faster.

On the snowy meadow, a class follows the instructor, weaving down slope in gentle curves. A boy appears at the crest of the mountain, between two snow-laden spruce trees. Behind him comes a girl. His skis lift as if by magic, trailing a feather of snow behind them.

The newly arrived skier can wait no longer. He tightens his boots quickly. He takes the skis off the car rack, rushes to the chaletlike lodge where they sell the tickets for the lifts, slips into his bindings, reaches for his ski poles. In long strides, he is at the lift. This one consists of chairs, which whisk him safely, easily off the ground.

Then he is being wafted upward, above the picturesque roofs. The valley and the parking lots disappear. Under him, ski poles glint. He turns his head: a lone skier is dancing a solo down the slope. A white spray is his wake.

The hill isn't large. This one is in Wisconsin, all of 500 feet down. Large or small, the de-

Atop the mountain, heartbeats quicken in anticipation of downhill run.

scent becomes the purest of pleasures, once you know how to ski. Some writers have compared it to sailing; here, too, wind and sun are the enduring pleasures.

But as the ski-buff knows, you can really do so much more on a mountain than on water. A lake is always flat, but a mountain falls steeply or gently, grows narrow or wide, dips for a short stretch, and rises suddenly. On the water, you depend on the speed of a boat; on snow, you determine your own pace.

You can go very fast—straight —in what skiers call a *schuss;* or you can soar, float into arcs. Your senses will come alive as you bank around a corner.

You triumph over your skis;

they do your bidding. The good skier can make his turn as long or short as he chooses; he can let a cornice lift him through the air, then stop almost on a dime. Or he can let gravity pull, and go into a racer's crouch. The mountain plucks at him, increasing his speed. As he raises his eyes, the chair-lift towers flash by, a reddish blur. Speed is joy.

Skiing is an ego builder. The crowd admires those who ski well, and they seldom lack company. But even if you're only a snow bunny, you meet new people. The beginners' slope is full of them.

Those who want to get away from it all find a mecca in

At last—the exciting descent. Kicking up powder is a part of the fun.

A few youngsters begin to practice the basic walking step on the level.

skiing. On a summit, the silence can be absolute. There is only the blue sky and the well-scrubbed trees and the peak. The air quickens your breath. There is no smog at the heights. Dust doesn't exist. There are no screeching cars, no sirens, no slamming doors, no clattering typewriters, no nagging parents, no criticizing bosses, no jostling crowds. There is only silence. The pure, clean world washes away worries. Problems vanish into thin air.

While you ski, you feel light-hearted. That's probably why there are millions of enthusiasts today. And why even those who earn their living from this sport still can't get enough of it. When there is fresh powder snow, ski instructors even on their days off, still dash out early to the slopes.

Doctors know much about the health aspects of skiing. That is why many physicians themselves ski until they are in their seventies. A sixty-year-old skier—who has devoted forty years to the mountains—has the arteries of a man of forty. His lungs, his heart, his muscles are in perfect shape. The human body isn't meant for loafing.

The fine machinery of circulation, nerves, glands works better with the stimulus of invigorating exercise.

At what age should a skier begin? In the Swiss villages and in the Rocky Mountains, children often get their first boards when they have barely learned to walk. Experts like Willy Schaeffler, the coach, feel that this is good. But he advises parents to take their three-year-olds out *only* in good weather. Small children must be warm and dry, or they will come to hate skiing. They don't understand big words about technique. They want to have fun instead. For them, skiing should be play.

There are all sorts of games for children under five. They can build a pyramid of ski poles and duck through. If you ski yourself, you can simply place the preschooler in front of your own legs and trace careful curves down the hill. In time, he will begin to imitate you. But never force him beyond his own pace.

There are special ski classes at most areas. Some have kindergartens on skis. Good in-

13

Ted Dutton, Aspen, Colorado

structors are warmhearted, humorous, encouraging, full of gusto. They know the exact limits of children, whose strength shouldn't be taxed. In class, a child can learn skiing even more quickly than an adult.

At what age is it time for ski-school lessons? "Not before the age of five or six," says Curt Chase, of the Aspen ski school. "At two, three, or four, the attention span is too short. There should be ski games only." Chase shares the belief of other famous ski-school directors, like Doug Pfeiffer and Sigi Engl, that youngsters love competition. Nowadays, there are races for children at many resorts.

Obviously, a child who skis will walk better in summer, and tire less easily in fall. And if he starts young, he will develop more courage, sturdiness and initiative than the nonskier. He will also improve his co-ordination and timing.

Naturally, skiing takes practice. It does not come naturally. You will learn most easily through lessons given by a certified instructor. For a child, four lessons are often enough. And the well-conditioned teenager has an easier time than the

Family practices skills together.

adult office worker. For all learners, there will be at first a fumbling, a blundering, and repeated falling. But on the slopes, even tangled tumblings are punctuated with laughter.

No doubt about it, the first day is the hardest. The beginner feels awkward with all the strange equipment strapped to his feet.

After a few times on the slopes, the snow bunny can usually stand up. He learns to walk on his skis, which no longer seem clumsy. He learns to herringbone up a hill, and to glide down a gentle incline without a fall. The next step is the snowplow, which becomes his brake. He tries the first turns. Climbing and traversing on skis become easy. The new exercises feel comfortable. Already the rewards—fresh strength and flexibility and balance—are felt in every fiber. Step by step, the skier gains confidence. Soon he no longer fears the T-bars, the chairlifts, the platterpulls and other mechanical means designed to take him uphill. At last, a magnificent mountain world has been opened up to him.

How about the average young college girl or secretary? Can she afford skiing? Is she too old to learn? Can she take up the sport?

Yes, even if she has not skied before. Even mothers in their forties have started to ski because the whole family did. Skiing is balance, timing, and coordination. It may take the mothers a bit longer than their daughters, but, *with instruction,* they ski after a few sessions.

A girl does not have to be particularly athletic to ski. And neither does a young man. For the beginner, skiing takes more muscle than swimming or ten-

Knowing how to fall is essential.

Swiss National Tourist Office

Bill Schmid

Snow bunnies (top) take time out to feed their hardy appetites. Despite all the snow (bottom), the sun is warm enough for a siesta out of doors.

Swiss National Tourist Office

Arapahoe Basin Inc., Colorado

A brisk atmosphere, an attractive setting, and a challenging sport keep all the participants smiling.

nis; for the experienced—especially on a short slope—it takes no muscle at all; with the correct technique, the expert carves a graceful downhill route with no more effort than knifing through soft butter. One of America's best-known physicians for skiers puts it this way: "By and large, the physical demands of skiing can be met by most people."

The person who pursues summer activities—especially hiking —has a much easier time when winter comes. And it is absolutely essential for a young working girl *to get into condition before the snow falls.*

An hour's calisthenics twice a week, or fifteen minutes of gym-nastics a day will provide adequate physical strength for skiing. One expert suggests fourteen days of ten-minute sessions. Specifically, you can strengthen your legs with half-knee bends— that is, not all the way down. To improve stomach muscles, sit-ups are good. Young people can also try waddling like ducks —forward, backward, right and left—hands on hips. Some skiers prefer cycling in fall to develop leg strength. You can use the bongo board for balance, rope-skipping for agility and timing. Walk instead of driving, whenever possible.

It's amazing how little time it takes to get ready for skiing. Nor do you have to work out like a super-athlete. In fact, physical education teachers will tell you that exercise must be increased gradually, and without strain.

Good conditioning is the best safeguard against skiing accidents. Fit people are less likely to get hurt. You only have to look at a downhill race. Skiers barrel down a steep hill at tremendous speeds—most of them completely safe.

Just how dangerous is skiing? For those who use judgment

17

Safe skiers are happy skiers. Obey danger signs posted by the officials!

and common sense, it is no more risky than other sports. Medical surveys at Mt. Snow, Vermont, Sun Valley, Idaho, and Vail, Colorado, have given most of the statistical answers to conjecture about accidents. The National Ski Patrol, whose volunteers roam the slopes with first-aid belts and toboggans, has also kept track of skiing safety figures for almost thirty years.

The picture is more cheerful than you might think. Four to six skiers in 1,000 are injured. Of these, only a third suffer a broken bone. The rest have sprains or cuts and bruises. And more likely than not, it's their own fault.

You can't expect to get into condition on a skiing holiday. You have to do it before. You shouldn't ski when you're tired or famished. You shouldn't ski beyond your ability. You should never, under any circumstances, use faulty equipment.

The surveys also tell us that the first days are the most dangerous. Thereafter, the peril comes chiefly for those who ski out of control. The more one skis in a season, the less chance for injuries. Instructors who are on the slopes every day will seldom wind up in first-aid rooms, even less often in hospitals.

What else can you do to reduce the risk? Join a ski class—especially before your first few days out on the slopes. Instructors grade their students with a knowing eye, and you'll seldom be sent to a hill beyond your skills. Instructors go slow when the snow or the light is bad; the good ones watch over their students like mother hens. Best of all, they nudge the skier into keeping his equipment in safe working order.

Why ski? For the joy, the strength gained, the satisfaction of a disciplined body instantly obeying the mind's commands. For the sensation, unlike any other, of sheer physical prowess, of cutting through air and space and sky gracefully, beautifully—a sensation as near as man comes to that of a bird in flight.

Aspen Association

With skis, poles, goggles and gloves, you're ready for any kind of slope!

Chapter Two

EQUIPMENT AND LESSONS:
MUSTS AND MAYBES

Modern skiers can count their blessings when it comes to the quality of today's ski equipment. However, they must also count their dollars: good ski gear has become expensive.

It wasn't that way forty years ago. In those days skiers used long, wooden slats that curved high at the tip and looked a little like the bow of a ship. The wood was thick and weighed a lot. It took effort to make the ski turn in the snow. Youngsters often skied on barrel staves. The bindings that held their boots to the skis were simple—just a group of leather straps. (Some skiers used thick rubber canning-jar washers or even rope.) The ski poles were little more than thick wooden staffs.

Twenty years ago the rough cloth of ski clothing and the unshapely windbreakers were characteristic; they flapped and rustled as skiers came down the mountain. A scarf was usually around the sportsman's neck, waving like a flag behind him. But at least all his gear cost him very little.

Skis have now become a thing of beauty. They're streamlined, tapered, rounded at the tips. They are calculated by engineers to the fraction of an inch. They've been fitted with sharp offset steel edges that bite the snow. Beginners no longer have to do much fancy waxing. Modern skis come with excellent plastic bottoms. Some paraffin over the plastic coating will do for most novices.

Machines have been invented

that can compute a ski's behavior. Ski manufacturers test and re-test their products for the ability to turn in all kinds of snow and at all speeds.

Metal skis have taken over. Today, skis are complicated sandwiches of many materials: rare aluminum alloys, glued portions of fine woods, plastics or rubber.

Even wooden skis now consist of several layers of wood. This gives the ski greater strength. Although the wooden skis still break more easily than those made of metal, the better hickories are lively, bouncy and resilient. What's more, prices of wooden skis ($30. to $100.) are not quite as high as the metal ones. The beginner does just as well with wooden skis if he gets a flexible pair. (Stiff skis are for racers.) Nor do beginners need "competition" skis.

Recently, still another space-age invention appeared: a plastic ski. It can be made of expensive resins (like tree saps). These are called "epoxies," and can cost up to $200. Fiberglass skis run from $30. to $100. The better plastic skis are pliable. They adapt themselves beautifully to any terrain.

All the new lightweight skiing equipment handles easier and is much simpler to get on and off.

Experience has shown that, for the average skier, metal skis are most durable. (Note that under the hard-hitting feet of racers, the metal sandwich has been known to come apart.) Beginners and intermediates love them, because the skis will slide with a dreamlike quality, except on ice. Here, metal skis can make terrible noises and often wander in the wrong direction. Not all expert skiers—at least not those skiers who like to go straight and fast—are convinced that metal is for them. At high speeds, they say, metal doesn't "track" as well as wood.

The best metal skis can cost from $95. to $150. If you're not rich, you can save money by asking for any ski make *which is discounted.* Some famous domestic makes of metal skis are fair-traded, *which means that you'll never get a price break.* You can buy a discounted pair of $125. metal skis for $80. if the dealer feels in the mood, or if he hopes to get your future business on other items, or is closing out his winter wares.

On the other hand, be sure you receive a guarantee from the store for whatever discounted brand of metal skis you buy. This certificate assures you that you'll get a new pair (or a free repair) if the skis do not stand up. Guarantees should be for at least a year.

Another important tip: *Try to buy your skis in a big city.* In small towns, where there is only one ski equipment outlet, you will have to pay whatever is asked. But in large cities there is real competition among the stores. Some skiers have gone to buy their outfits at the last minute at a ski area far away from a town. To their disappointment, prices were stiff. But even in the city you must compare carefully. The biggest bargains (but no service) can sometimes be found at discount stores, department stores, and large sporting-goods shops. Specialty stores—which only handle ski equipment in the winter—are generally more expensive, but they are also more reliable and knowledgeable. You're safest in a shop which has been in business for a long time.

The shop can also help you find the proper length of ski for you. It varies, but a good rule is that the ski should run from the ground to about your wrist when your arm is raised over your head. You can add a couple of inches if you're heavy, or take off a few inches if you're thin. The trend among non-athletic beginners is toward shorter skis. But this doesn't mean the short short ski, which is really only a toy.

Skis for children should not be much taller than they are. Tots do best with short soft boards. A pre-schooler can learn on hand-me-downs, if they're not too warped. Or the beginner can get an inexpensive Japanese ski outfit for about $15. Under no circumstances should you let the salesman talk you into a fancy pair of skis for a child just beginning. Unless you are wealthy, you should reserve this purchase for a future date.

23

The safety bindings of this type will release a skier's boot under pressure, to insure user's safety.

Boots should be stiff, fit snug, and must be strapped securely to skis to insure the user's safety.

Snap lock releases at skier's heel, is fine for the advanced skier, but not for beginners.

Used equipment will often do for adult beginners who are unsure of how many times they will ski, or for military people who may soon be transferred out of ski areas.

A word of caution: Wooden skis should not be left in the snow overnight, or they will age too fast. And metal or plastic skis don't belong next to the hot stove for any length of time. For summer storage, experienced skiers stand their skis on the tails, not tips. A block of wood or cork goes in the center between the strapped-together surfaces. This helps the ski keep its bounce.

At the end of the season, a drop of oil should also be squirted into the bindings.

You know, of course, that the binding is the device that holds the boot to the ski. There are many types of bindings. They now have automatic release features built into them: If you fall, extreme pressure is applied to the mechanism, and it opens. Some bindings release your heel if you spill; others open laterally—that is, on the side; and a third type releases the front of the boot. There are also combinations of these.

What makes for an ideal binding? "Trouble-free performance," says Earl Miller, a manufacturer. And, "It [the device] should be easy to put on." Miller recommends a snap-lock type which attaches the boot to the ski at both toe and heel. You can just step into this one using the ski pole in most cases. Miller also says there should be several angles of pull on the binding by the foot, at which the snap-lock catch releases the boot. "If you have less than five angles, it's like buying a para-

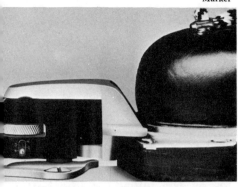

Before buying any safety bindings, particularly for a child, be sure they fit the wearer's weight.

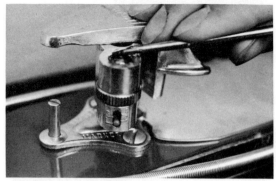

Oil the mechanisms before packing ski bindings away. This will keep them trouble free.

chute that only opens part of the time."

Children should get a binding designed for their exact *weight*. A child may take only one-tenth the pressure in releasing the ski as an adult. Step-in types save the parents' patience.

Most racers prefer turntables that don't really turn, plus a "long thong" made of a long leather strap, which roots them to the ski. These bindings are dangerous for the new skier. The most famous race bindings are made by Marker. They are so well known that when they open by mistake—which doesn't happen often—angry racers say they "markered out."

Bindings cost from $10. to $30. Whether you can afford it or not, you should get good ones. They may save a broken leg. After the first adjustment by the store, it's really up to

you to keep the binding in good order. As you know, it should open when you fall. You should see that all screws are tight. If there are cables, make sure you haven't worn them out. The binding should come with a special leather "safety" strap that attaches to your boot. Runaway skis are deadly things, and some areas *insist* on the use of the safety straps.

Any spill can be dangerous unless you wear a safety binding that automatically releases as you fall. Sun Valley News Bureau

Today's skiers seem to prefer the buckle-type single boot to the laced double boot pictured above.

You will also need poles for skiing. (The British still call them "sticks," to remind us of the past.) Modern poles are magnificent instruments. They are light, hollow, balanced, and tapered toward the bottom. The aluminum alloys and steel prove the most popular materials. All poles have a grip. The best ones are molded to your fingers. The pole has a leather wrist strap, a metal shaft that glints in the sun, a small, basketlike snowguard made of plastic or rubber, and a steel tip that should be sharp enough to stab the snow but not so sharp as to hurt someone. Poles start from $5. and go to $26. for an Idaho-made masterpiece. Proper length? About to your armpit.

Modern ski boots are de-signed for maximum efficiency. An inner boot holds your foot in a snug grip; an outer boot keeps the water from coming through. Boots now have buckles on the outside. Some better boots have hidden hinges that give the skier a chance to lean forward as he skis. Boots are only as good as their fit. They cost anywhere from $30. to $190. (the latter for handmade *Aspen* boots—the world's most expensive).

Ski-boot soles are stiff. Check them for wear and tear once in awhile. It's not pleasant if the heel comes off just as you start to demonstrate your downhill technique. Boots preserve best in a boot-tree, just as clothes belong on a hanger.

Boots have a lot to do with your skiing—even for beginners. Loose boots are dangerous because your feet can't control the skis. The ankle should have no play; the heel should be well cupped, and the sides must give support; the toes must have room to wiggle—or they'll get numb from the cold.

Should a child get a new pair of boots every year? Experts disagree on that point; but if you're short on cash, buy a size larger. If they're too big, an extra pair of socks and an inner sole may help. Rubber boots over regular shoes won't do.

How about socks? A thin pair first, with a woolen pair on top, should do. For youngsters, socks must be small and double-checked for wrinkles: sensitive skin blisters fast. Baby powder is good for tender feet.

Most salesmen say a youngster should get a new pair of ski pants every year because he has outgrown the old one. Pants, like a parka, should last for several winters. In the Alps, farm children ski to school through bad weather in home-made or inherited ski togs.

Ski pants don't make the skier, but a pair of $65. stretch pants looks handsome, especially on an attractive, slender girl. For those who can afford it, there are fashionable children's ski clothes in the shops these days. Patterns differ little from those for adults: well-padded, warm parkas; taut pants.

Long underwear, flannel or cotton shirts, sweaters, and a cap or headband will complete the skier's basic winter wardrobe. Don't forget mittens—mountains can chill you to the

Warm, lightweight clothing is best.

Equipment is costly. Rent it until you're sure that this sport is for you.

bone. Goggles for a snow storm are a *must;* and bring a pair of shatter-proof glasses for protection against the sun.

One final point about ski equipment: If you want to try the sport, you don't have to *buy* everything. You can rent skis, poles and boots for $2. to $5. per day. You may be asked for credit identification, especially in the area rental shops.

If you want to ski for the whole season, you can get a special plan. Some city shops will let you rent equipment for around $50. If you're enthusiastic, this fee runs from the time when the first flakes fall to the moment when the flowers begin to show above the last patches of snow.

Once you're equipped, it's only a snowball's throw to the ski-school desk. Should you take lessons or shouldn't you?

For first-timers, the answer is

clear. A first lesson will spare several long, otherwise grueling solo sessions. Most teachers have the patience of angels with the beginner.

Instructors will check to see that your equipment fits and operates. They're willing to give you advice if you need to buy some new things.

It's remarkable how fast the ski instructor can teach you. By the end of the first day, you'll have learned to walk on the level, to get up when you fall, to climb a small hill and to ski down a short, gentle slope.

Most schools have adopted the American technique. This means you can ski at several resorts and get the same type of instruction. For a beginner, four full-day lessons are recommended by such famous ski-school directors as Doug Pfeiffer or Curt Chase. Inter-

28

mediate skiers should brush up their technique at the beginning of the season, and the expert should refine his skiing in a class. If you are on vacation, you can save money by buying a full week's ski-school ticket. Individual lessons are extremely expensive; for group lessons, you pay from $6. to $12. for a morning and afternoon session.

Is ski school really important? According to the National Ski Patrol, it is: Injured skiers have usually *not* been in a class. Some schools give as many as 50,000 lessons a season. And all American schools have worked out foolproof systems of teaching.

What's the best and quickest way to learn skiing basics? Take lessons!

Experts show perfect downhill form—knees bent, shoulders forward.

Chapter Three

THE ABC's OF SKIING

On cold winter days, the ski-school bell rings cheerily. The time: 10:00 A.M. for the morning session and 1:30 P.M. for the afternoon. Skiers have bought their tickets, and are now rushing toward the lesson area. How do they carry their skis? They shoulder them, tips forward. The poles are hooked under the backs of the skis. The skiers are careful to get through crowds without hitting anyone or stepping on anyone else's skis or poles. Ski-school directors and instructors are already assembled, eager to put each person in the right class. A few questions are enough for the teacher to determine the skier's ability. No one need feel self-conscious about being a first-timer. Many, many years

ago, the tanned, lean ski-school chief stepped onto *his* skis for the first time. If the beginner is a boy, he shouldn't be surprised to have a woman instructor. She's capable, or she wouldn't be there. For teaching children, nine times out of ten she is better than a man.

"This way!" says the instructor, going to a flat area, lining up the class. For first-timers the teacher will help with their bindings. Are they well adjusted? Does the boot sit well on the ski? Boot and ski should really make one unit. Are the boot-laces hanging all over the place? Are the boots tight? Is the strap on? Good.

The instructor may begin by explaining how wonderfully useful ski poles are. Without them,

Bending the knees and ankles without falling isn't as easy as it looks.

a skier couldn't get up a hill. Poles assist in turns and help a skier to stride on the level. The instructor will now demonstrate how to walk on skis. It's as simple as walking without skis and is learned quickly. Just slide one ski after the other across the snow. The teacher repeats the famous cry: "Bend ankles and knees!" Knees definitely should be bent slightly while walking. And rhythm is all-important: Right ski and left pole forward, then left ski and right pole.

The first lesson has started!

Now comes the step-turn which allows the skier to change direction. The snow tracks left by this simple maneuver look like the spokes of a wheel. In a standing position, the teacher will ask the learner to place the left leg a few inches to the left. The right leg follows. And so on until a half circle has been completed. The circle is then reversed. Right leg a few inches to the right, left leg following. In this simple fashion, the skier learns balance, gains confidence, and acquires the first sense of changing direction.

Now comes a first lesson in climbing. Could a skier go

straight up a hill, skis together? Of course not; the skis would slide backward. Instead, the teacher will climb up the hill obliquely. He climbs step by step, never too steeply. "Here the poles are very important," he'll say. "Use them!"

As the beginner tries it, he will notice for the first time why his skis have steel edges, and why they should be sharpened by a ski shop once a year. The edges hold on the slippery, mounting surface of the hill. The weight of the body is always on the lower ski in the climb. At the top of the first hill, the triumphant learner will feel like a conqueror of Everest and, after a little while, just as tired! That's when he first discovers why skiers should be in condition.

The instructor may next demonstrate a herringbone. It's a good word, for the ski tracks will later look exactly like the skeleton of a fish. This maneuver is a second and faster way to get uphill. See the expert do it: He spreads his ski tips to a wide angle, and plants the poles firmly on the outside, behind the bindings. Standing erect, he lifts one ski and places

Everyone must learn how to walk before he can ski. Try to develop a smooth and rhythmic movement.

it upward. The edges dig in, and the poles do their work, supporting his weight. Then he lifts the other ski and it too goes up. He continues to climb in this fashion. If done for long, herringboning becomes strenuous. For this reason, the beginner is told to practice it on his own.

Meanwhile, he learns something easier: the downhill position. The ankles and knees are bent, and the shoulders are slightly forward. Poles are kept behind. The body weight should be forward. In fact, a basic rule is: *The steeper the hill, the farth-*

33

A fishlike pattern marks the snow as skiing group herringbones to top of the snow-covered mountain.

er forward the skier should lean.

Ready? Now coast downhill. If the ankles and knees are bent and the weight is squarely over the skis, balance can be kept. There is no reason to fall. If a skier does tumble, he does so *lightly.* Experienced skiers don't tense or stiffen. Once he has fallen, a learner is given a good rule to get up by: The skis must first be parallel. Don't point tips or tails downhill; instead, get the skis into a horizontal position. Then push up to a standing position.

Now the kick turn is taught. It's a useful way of turning in the opposite direction. The kick turn is done *while standing*, and with full help of the poles. The right pole goes forward, left one to the rear. Now the left ski is lifted, swings around until it is parallel with the right ski, facing in the opposite direction. As you lean on your poles, your right ski can now join the left.

The snowplow is next on the list. Some ski schools look down on the plow as too pedestrian, but it's really the best invention for slowing down and stopping. Novices who have learned how to snowplow are far ahead of the game.

The instructor doesn't attempt a verbal description of this maneuver. He'll *show it*. Then he'll have the learner repeat it until it can be done smoothly. Difficult? Hardly. The tips of the skis are almost together and the tails apart, forming a V. Again, just as in the downhill position, the ankles are bent. When the inside edges of the skis dig in, your speed is diminished. The more the edges dig in, the slower the speed. The snowplow is a fine brake for the beginner. The better the skier, the flatter the skis will be on the snow, the less the snowplow will be needed.

For the rest of the lesson, the instructor will most likely alternate between the snowplow and straight running: he will spread the tails of his skis and then bring them together again. "Don't get your tips crossed," he'll warn.

A beginner will find that ski instruction follows a logical system. One exercise simply grows into the next. For instance, the snowplow will be followed by the snowplow turn. When it is mastered, and the use of a ski tow is learned, the skier can roam all over the beginners' hill.

How does the teacher achieve a snowplow turn? He does it by shifting his weight. While making a snowplow, he drops his left shoulder and—because of the law of inertia — he turns to the right. Again, his knees are bent. He will demonstrate how to keep turning—right, left, right, left—all the way down a slope. The tips of his skis are always in a V position, but the V is open at the bottom.

A beginner should not wait too long before taking his next lesson! As with any student, he may forget what he has learned. Most teachers will instruct a new skier early how to traverse. This is not difficult. Traversing a hill on skis is a little like traversing, or crossing, a street, except that the hill slopes downward. Your skis are together, but most of the weight is *on the downhill ski*. The skier leans downhill from the hip, and meanwhile his upper body, even his head, tilts up the slope. With this weight distribution, the lower ski edge bites sharply into the snow.

The stem turn is next. "It has a great advantage over the snowplow turn," says Curt

First rule: Don't be stiff. Relax!

Chase of the Aspen ski school. "It can be executed on much steeper hills." A stem turn is really half a snowplow. The skier starts it in a traverse, with knees flexed. He energetically transfers his weight from the downhill ski to the uphill ski. If he does this fast, he has a stem christie, where both feet are brought together again. The secret of success? Ask any instructor. Relax! Once a skier tenses up, his motions will become more jerky, and he will tire more easily.

The instructor will first let a skier christie across the slope and then *uphill*. The beginner soon discovers that the faster he goes, the easier it is to turn! And, strangely enough, he always leans left when he wants to go right. Doesn't seem logical? Yet you only have to attach an object—say your ballpoint pen—to a piece of string. Twist the string as far as it will go. Now let the pencil start to dance. You'll see that it "untwists" in the opposite direction. The same thing should be done with an advanced ski turn: the shoulder must always go in the direction opposite to the turn.

Many skiers stop taking lessons after they can stem downhill. They can then master all but the most difficult runs. At this point, a skier will move into other dimensions: He is a bird, swooping from the sky; he is a sailor on a vast, white ocean; he is an explorer venturing onto new trails—Peary at the North Pole, Byrd in the Antarctic. The cold no longer is bothersome. He wears goggles and doesn't mind the falling snows. Ski clothes keep out the wind. He discovers the deliciousness of spring skiing. The melting snow will seem all the faster, and people will praise his tan complexion. A word of caution: The spring sun is strong on snow. A screening agent of some sort is needed: good tan-

Class of young boys learns the proper way to get on feet after a spill.

Wide World Photos

ning lotion or cream will be fine for the dark-haired; blonds may need a protective cream. Take a chapstick or zinc ointment along, too. Lips blister.

And now is the time to go back to school. A skier can now note all the more clearly how schools plan every step with care, how they lead a learner smoothly from one step to the next. A famous instructor like Willy Schaeffler, who has coached at Denver University for many years, will show every movement *in slow motion.* He can tell just why each move is done in a certain way, then correct mistakes.

A skier at this level of proficiency will make many mistakes as he learns parallel skiing. The dictionary says that "parallel" means "evenly in the same direction." This also describes the skis: They are so close to each other in parallel skiing that a dollar bill can be put between boots and held there. The skis start together. And they turn together, knees locked. It is worth asking an expert to show this technique. It can be a handsomely controlled movement.

Parallel skiing is also the basis for the short swing, which lives up to its name. A lot of quick, short swings down the hill are called "wedeln." This is a German word meaning tail-wagging. Wedeln takes talent, lots of practice, and application.

According to Curt Chase, all these maneuvers also require a fine sense of balance, coordina-

French Tourist Office

Skiers increase racing speed by bending farther and farther forward.

U.S. Army

Stowe News Bureau

Kick turn (above, left) and snowplow (below) are not as difficult as they seem, but the man (above, right) needs more practice in stopping.

Wide World Photos

38

Swiss National Tourist Office

In traversing (above), the trick is to lean away from the hill. To stem turn (below), flex knees and shift weight from downhill to uphill ski.

Wide World Photos

39

40

Mastering comma position of Pepi Gramshammer takes years of practice.

tion, timing, and *feeling*. More speed is needed for these figures than for a stem.

"Parallel skiing is the advanced stage of the sport," Curt Chase explains. "Now the instructor becomes a coach who makes the student feel the motions and rhythms."

Parallel skiing means "leg action" turns. The whole body —especially the shoulders—leans far out, sitting above the hill just like a comma. This is called "angulation." The upper body moves into the opposite direction of the turn, which is called counter-rotation. The most important work is done by the legs —especially by the ankles, which are always bent. For parallel skiing and short swings, the poles come in handy to help in turning. The skis are flat from one arc to the next. Edges are used only briefly as the weight shifts from one turn to another.

Schools that have been directed in various parts of the United States and Canada by Doug Pfeiffer and Miki Hutter lead to these advanced turns by hopping. Then they show the down-up-down motions. Before long, a skier will master the "heel thrust," which gives him the power to swivel around without effort.

After he gains confidence, he will find steep slopes a challenge. For a good skier, these are no longer frightening. On the contrary, they make skiing much easier for the experienced.

Some skiers have learned wedeln in a single season. Many find it takes them a couple of winters or longer. Others are content with their stem christies. Along the way, they will all learn to cope with every kind of snow. In deep snow, for example, they will sit back a bit more. Through trial and error, they will realize that deep powder has to be treated gently, for "snow does not forgive," as a Frenchman put it. They will be especially careful on "breakable crust." This is a tricky kind of snow: its frozen surface can cave in as the skier crosses it. They will handle ice by leaning forward even more and using the edges. Faster and faster they will go, "respecting" or following the "fall line," which means the straightest way down. Experts are always in control of their skis. This means safety for everybody—the skier himself, his companions and the spectators.

Chair lifts give skiers opportunity to take pleasure in winter beauty.

Chapter Four

WHERE TO GO SKIING

Skiing costs money. But we've seen that you can shave dollars on equipment if you're a beginner. Stick to discounted and less advertised brands. Shop intelligently: compare! Or begin with used gear, letting an experienced friend help you choose it. Naturally, new skis and accessories are priced highest just before the start of the season and lowest at the time everyone thinks of golf, swimming and fishing. That's the time to make the rounds; salesclerks will be glad to see you. For used equipment, scan the classified ads in your home town papers and try the rental shops, which sometimes sell used items.

How do you cut the high prices of ski instruction in the main ski areas of the United States? (In Europe, lessons cost only half as much.) The solution is a ski school in your own city. Many newspapers advertise and even offer classes at a reasonable rate. They do the latter for the sake of promoting their paper. In Denver, the *Rocky Mountain News* charges only $9. for six excellent lessons. Classes are held there for all levels, with a maximum of fifteen pupils, although there are as many as 1,700 pupils in all. In Salt Lake City, the *Deseret News Telegram* has an excellent program; and in Cleveland, the well-known *Plain Dealer* now gives lessons to 6,000 skiers every season. If you live near Chicago, you should consider the *Chicago Tribune's* ski school, which is free. In Seattle, the city itself manages an

43

For beginners, gentle slopes near home provide the best practice.

excellent learn-to-ski week. Of course, you will have to register for these schools when they are announced. Most programs fill up quickly. YMCA's, YWCA's and ski clubs also organize schools.

This leads to another corner-cutter: Clubs often have senior members who will teach you for the fun of it. They are not certified instructors, but advanced skiers who get pleasure out of doing their share.

Many clubs will charter buses throughout the winter, or they organize car pools. Here you share the cost or the effort of driving. Clubs also use trains and planes. A Texas club regularly moves its members to Aspen for a week end, and one club in Boston even arranges a yearly flight to ski in Australia! Some clubs have their own chalets in the mountains, where members

can stay at very reasonable prices.

Clubs vary, of course. If you live in Denver, there is the Eskimo Club, which consists of youngsters from nine years to seventeen. Every Saturday, thousands of the Eskimos board a special ski train to Winter Park. A club like this one is good for young people whose parents don't ski, because they get instruction and chaperoning at a very low cost.

New skiers start with basic steps performed on the level. As boys and girls improve, they are advanced to gentle hills where they are taught the next steps. By degrees, they are promoted from level to practice hill, then to the tows, to beginner trails, to intermediate trails, and finally to the advanced areas. Each step along the way is marked by a test. Each test that is passed means a colored badge

Vermont Development Department

Smaller areas still use rope tows.

Vail Publicity

to wear on the left sleeve. If the test is failed, it means more practice and another try. Generally, it takes several ski seasons to attain the advanced color badge.

The Eskimos and some other clubs also have sensible arrangements for renting equipment. After all, people under seventeen are still growing, so the rental idea can work out well. Denver is typical: There are 60-odd clubs, a group to fit almost everyone's special needs. Most larger cities near the "ski belts" have a similar variety.

Dues go anywhere from zero to $10. a year and up. To get the name of the club nearest you, write to the U.S. Ski Association, Broadmoor Hotel, Colorado Springs; or to one of the divisional association offices in other areas. Once you're sold on skiing, it is also a good idea to

Western slopes offer longer runs.

join the USSA. (One of its advantages: a low ski insurance.)

You can reduce the cost of skiing in other ways. For example, ski tickets are cheaper by the season if you ski more than twenty-five times. Many areas have a family rate. Some will even let a skier under twelve ski free if he brings a parent along. And remember, half-day tickets are always lower than the all-day ones. Spend the morning in the sunshine or climb on your skis.

When you first start to ski, you need not travel far to enjoy the sport. Many young people go to a city park or to a golf course. For a beginner, the gently rolling hills and the lack of other skiers can be far more pleasant than the crowded, faraway ski area. In a city park, you will have to herringbone uphill. This is work but it's rewarding, too. You strengthen your legs for the rest of the season.

After you become more skillful, you may want to try a cross-country trip on skis with friends or your family. It's another fine way of saving money while skiing. You will gain a closer acquaintance with na-

ture and you will speed up your body conditioning.

The time will come when you will want to do as much downhill skiing as possible. (Ski-school director Doug Pfeiffer calls this period the "downhill madness.") At this point, you should use the ski tows. They're convenient because they take you to the mountaintop fast and without effort, and in this way you can ski more runs in a day. If your hours are precious and you long to improve your technique fast, ski tows are indeed the answer. Uphill conveyances are built at a fantastic rate all over North America, and many areas have actually doubled the number of their lifts, adding new ones every year.

Are ski tows dangerous? Not according to *Ski Area Management* Magazine, which has made many studies of ski lifts. Even freak accidents are rare. Operators are paid to help the novice, and the ski patrol is always willing to help. Remember, too, that the Forest Service and other United States agencies watch over the safety of each lift.

You will encounter several types of ski lifts. The most popular right now is the double-chair lift. It is tailored for good companionship; you meet many new people here. Although you cannot move, the chairs are not as cold as you would think: Two people usually shield one another from the wind. Some operators provide woolen ponchos with hoods to protect skiers from the wind that sweeps the mountain. Several areas have also installed lifts that seat three people in a row. It's easy to get onto such a lift. Grab your pole shafts in one hand, look behind to see the chair approaching, and just sit down.

Another way of moving up the hill is the T-bar. Beginners can use it after only a few ski lessons, but don't try it the first time on skis. Your legs won't be able to cope with the unevenness of the mountain. This conveyance lives up to its name. It has a bar, which looks like an upside-down T. It rides two people. An operator puts the bar under your seat. You lean against it, hold onto a center pole, and slide upward.

A Poma lift works on the same principle, except that it loads only one person for each bar. There has a sort of round dish instead of the "T" for the

seat. That's why it is sometimes called a "platter pull."

Rope tows, which still dot many of the small areas, take muscle to use, for you have to hold onto the rope on your way up the hill. Tighten your grip slowly. Fortunately, rope tow hills are seldom very long or steep. And after awhile you will learn the trick of squeezing the rope under your arms. Never wear loose, flappy clothing *or a scarf* when riding a rope tow. And don't be afraid that you'll be eaten up by the machinery on top: there is an automatic safety device for those who hang on beyond a certain point.

Another way of reaching a summit is by gondola. This is an enclosed steel or plastic cabin that allows two, four, or more passengers to take off their skis for the uphill ride. Gondolas hang from cables. This transportation is catching on in the States just as it did in the Alps years ago. At one Vermont area, there is even a gondola for the lazy passenger. This unique cabin takes you all the way to the top with your skis on!

We'll soon take a look at the individual "areas." What does the term mean? An area may

Skimobile ride is a luxurious one.   *Dorms are crowded, but less costly.*

consist of many banded-together hills, complete with uphill machinery, ski schools, warming shacks, cafeterias and restaurants, nurseries, piped-in music. Before getting to some of the areas famous in the country —among which are holiday resorts like Sun Valley—let's first visit the various American ski regions.

According to the U.S. Ski Association, we can now ski in thirty-five of our fifty states, and this includes skiing on two 13,000-foot-high volcanoes in Hawaii. (These are called Mauna Lea and Mauna Loa.) There's little skiing in the South. There is some skiing near Gatlinburg, Tennessee; and because Texans like the sport so much, they have several ski shops. Throughout the Southwest, the picture is varied. New Mexico boasts no less than eight ski areas, and Arizona has three. There is no skiing to speak of in Oklahoma and Arkansas or in South Carolina, but North Carolina has a number of spots for ski enthusiasts.

Actually, there are five major American ski regions.

One: The East, which includes the highly developed New England one and the Eastern seaboard. It could also be called "Skiboard," for you will find many areas in New York state, New Jersey, and there is even skiing at the "Homestead" in Virginia. The snow sometimes descends late on the rolling, wooded hills of Maine, New Hampshire, and Vermont, but

Swiss-style buildings add to the charm of this lovely Sun Valley resort.

the unbelievably numerous ski tows make up for the lost time. Thanks to snowmaking, Connecticut and Massachusetts now also have skiing.

Two: The Midwest, where you not only ski in the cold temperatures of Michigan, but also in Wisconsin, Minnesota, the Dakotas, and at Ski Pal, Iowa.

Three: The Rocky Mountains, which (unlike the Midwest) are distinguished by high mountains, long descents and long seasons. The Rockies include Colorado, Wyoming, Utah, Montana and, in Canada, Alberta and British Columbia.

Four: The West. Many areas in California, some in Nevada.

Five: The Pacific Northwest. This area includes Oregon and Washington, where summer skiing is possible on the glaciers. Since we spoke earlier of Canada, we should not forget the provinces of Ontario, Manitoba and, most of all, Quebec, with its picturesque, winter-shrouded Laurentians. Naturally, Alaska is also a U.S. ski country.

What is the "best" ski area and where is it? What should it offer? What features must you look for? It depends on your age, taste, evening plans and, of course, your skill as a skier. The better you become, the more you will be attracted by long runs and good snow conditions. You will also demand variety in the terrain. Instead of the Green Mountains, the White Mountains or the Catskills, you will clamor for the Rockies.

T-bar lifts can be very dangerous. No tyro should attempt to hitch a ride on one without first being shown the proper way to use it.

Vermont Development Department

Yet a ski holiday in the Midwest can be perfect for the beginner or the older person who doesn't need such swift descents. Snow-making now makes it possible to ski even in the South. The majority of older skiers demand comfort and a resort with many new hotels, motels and restaurants which are springing up in the "ski belts." (The smaller areas do not have this wide choice.) If you are on holiday, you may also feel that evening entertainment is important. The small areas in this country have few places where you can dance, frolic, or see a show; so for these, you will do better at the larger and more famous places.

Let us take the better-known areas alphabetically, starting with Alta, Utah. This spot is paradise for the skier who seeks the quiet of gigantic mountains. Alta consists of only a few small hotels wedged deep in a valley, endless stretches of powder snow, and almost no trees. Intermediate skiers now have their own trails.

Aspen, Colorado, 207 miles from Denver, needs no introduction.

By car, you go via the Loveland Basin and Arapahoe Basin

ski areas. Or you can fly. This takes only thirty minutes from Denver, and gives you a good chance to see that Aspen now has three well developed ski mountains: Ajax, topping the town itself, Aspen Highlands and Buttermilk Mountain. Aspen is also developing the gigantic snowmass area. In all, you can ski over a terrain of 130 miles, choose one of the available 5,000 beds in every price range, and learn to ski at Curt Chase's ski school—one of the world's largest.

Banff, Canada, has such fine skiing facilities that it just missed getting the Olympic Games. Your quickest way to the long, fast trails is to fly to Calgary. Banff is also headquarters for a national park, the Canadian Alpine Club and the magnificent Canadian Rockies.

Big Bromley, Vermont, can't boast a 12,000-foot altitude. But there are some forty instructors, 18 slopes, and a cafeteria that has room for 1,200 hungry people. The management of Big Bromley is interested in youngsters: there are special ski courses for children from six to eight, kindergarten for the younger ones, and season rates for juniors. If you have small brothers or sisters, they can be left at the nursery.

Big Mountain, Montana, also known as Whitefish, is a great place to escape the crowds. (Whitefish is the town eight miles to the north.) The Great Northern Railroad goes to this far-removed wonderland of snow formations that dazzle your eyes. It is said that the snow averages a depth of 96 inches at Big Mountain. You'll find every type of lift here and, in February, a winter carnival.

Boyne Mountain and Boyne Highlands, Michigan, are typical of Midwestern skiing in only one respect: the ski enthusiasm shows itself on week ends, when many people rush up North. During the week there are no waiting lines at the tows. Boyne has had some famous ski school directors, such as Stein Eriksen and Othmar Schneider. Boyne Falls, Harbor Springs, and Traverse City are not far away. Another Michigan ski area is Caberfae.

If you live in New York state, you should not miss a day at the new, modern, tow-rich area at Gore Mountain.

The Lake Placid region in

Skiers trek through the town of Aspen, Colorado, to the slopes of Ajax Mountain (in background).

New York state is one of the oldest American ski developments. There is the choice of four areas, and lots doing for people who like entertainment when they aren't skiing.

Jackson Hole, Wyoming, has opened its wide snow doors. An aerial tramway takes you up almost two miles (vertical drop: 4,135 feet), and you'll need good leg muscles to manage the long runs down the formidable Teton range! The cowboy food at Teton Village will taste all the better in the evening.

Mammoth Mountain is well-known to Californians for its manager and coach, Dave Mc-Coy. It has an elevation ranging up to 11,050, special half-price rates for children, and a long season, since it enjoys the late snows of the Sierras.

At Mount Baker, Washington, fifty-five miles from Bellingham, you ski all year. Students get special lift prices at this well-

Awesome vistas provide an extra

known spot, which boasts a glacier, a summer ski school, and the not-too-far-away ski riches of Mount Hood, Oregon. Here, too, a star-studded ski racing seminar takes place in summer. The coaches are Sailer, Molterer, Gramshammer, Spier and Schaeffler.

Mont Tremblant, at St. Jovite in the Canadian province of

52

is Solitude in Utah, and Sugar Bowl in California. The greatest ski attraction in California, however, is Squaw Valley, where the Olympic Winter Games took place in 1960. There are now fifteen ski lifts at Squaw Valley, and twenty-five runs—many for intermediate skiers. Squaw can best be reached via Reno, Nevada.

Sun Valley, Idaho, built in 1936, has had three decades of experience in pleasing its often difficult guests. Among them are movie stars, automobile tycoons, heads of governments, ski industry leaders. Prices can be high ($32. a night for a couple wanting a deluxe room with a balcony), but there are also dormitory beds for $3.50. For one and all, the two warm-water pools are free.

Stowe, Vermont, is the ski capital of the East. It is a typical New England village, complete with church spire and clean, white houses. But the new lodges, motels, guest homes, hotels and night clubs add a citylike touch of their own. Stowe is a busy place— even more so on week ends— but the many lifts can transport 6,000 people per hour up

Mount Mansfield and Spruce Peak. Stowe, Sun Valley, and Squaw Valley all try to offer as much as the great European ski resorts, which every American skier dreams of visiting.

Taos Ski Valley is the best-known ski area in New Mexico. It has been managed for a decade by Ernest Blake, who can also guide you to the secrets of the Taos Pueblo, where Indians still live as in the old days. A few Indians even ski down the steep, wooded New Mexican slopes.

Winter Park, Colorado, has long been the magnet for thousands of young people who go there every week end on the state's only ski train. (It doesn't run during the week.) On week days, Winter Park's seven jumping hills are generally deserted, and you can fly down one of the expert runs without fear of someone standing around the corner, or that you will be hit by the *schussboomers* on the intermediate trails. That's the time, too, when you will find room in the large cafeteria.

These are only a few of the best-known ski areas. In every major snow area, you will find some organized ski activity.

Downhill racer tucks tight, squeezes his poles securely under his arms.

Chapter Five

...PES OF
COMPETITION

Ski competitions are divided into Alpine and Nordic events. One type originated in the Alps; the other came from the Scandinavian countries.

Alpine means *slalom, giant slalom* and *downhill*. Nordic means *cross-country* and *jumping*, sometimes a combination of both. In the Olympics, these events also include a little-known competition called the "biathlon." This is for military people, who demonstrate their cross-country skiing technique and their accuracy with a rifle shooting at a target.

Women skiers compete in all events except jumping and the biathlon. Men seldom compete in both Nordic and Alpine fields, although some college skiers, aspiring to become "four-way" champions, will try. It is extremely difficult to excel in all ski events. It is something like expecting a 100-meter sprinter to run a marathon, or a skater to be equally good at ice hockey and speed skating.

Even the equipment is not the same for the Nordic and the Alpine skier. Cross-country skis are very narrow and light. They have bindings that let the heel move up and down. Their boots are soft. Jumping skis are heavy and longer, and have three (sometimes four) grooves for better control. Slalom skis are shorter than those for downhill. The curve under each type of ski varies, too. The degree of arching is called the "camber" of the ski. Experts are also interested in "side camber,"

57

Vail Publicity. Photo by Gerds

Shadows add to dangers of racing.

which influences the turn of the ski.

The efforts required at Nordic and Alpine tournaments are also quite different. A ski jumper is in the air only a short time and, though he may fly some 300 feet, his physical strength is used only briefly. A slalom racer must zoom through a series of flags. He has an explosive start and a tremendously demanding run, though it seldom takes more than a minute. The cross-country skier must have endurance, while the downhill skier needs leg power. The demands on skiers vary widely, as you can see.

But certain similarities exist in the characters of the competitors themselves. The better ones share a special drive that makes them practice hard to master technique. For serious competing, they need strength of will as much as physical strength. They are asked to give up over-eating, smoking, drinking. They must also sleep a regular number of hours.

When the would-be champion is just starting out, he may need willing parents or the will to work for money to supply his equipment. For the beginner,

Falls in slalom racing are frequent enough, but they're seldom serious.

no club, organization or manufacturer will pay the costs of contesting.

Serious ski competitors have something other than drive and willpower in common. Outwardly calm, they have a fire within them that makes the ski jumper take off at high speeds, and propels the slalom racer in a downhill rush. If the ski competitor does not have this inner daring, he will be crawling rather than roaring down a giant slalom course. Without this "fire," he belongs among the recreational skiers who en-

joy the sport in their own way. Not everyone is or should be a competitor.

The demands of competition increase tremendously on the national and international level. Top competitors *must* burn with thoughts of victory and have a do-or-die attitude. Men or women, they can think only of skiing, from the moment they wake to the instant they fall into bed at night. They long to take part in more and more ski meets. They observe each other, and when they see a movie, it probably has to do with skiing. 59

Contestants mass for start of popular cross-country race in Scandinavia.

Glide, kick—rhythmic step plus endurance make a cross-country skier.

Olympic skiers are often asked to forget their private lives. Coaches demand sacrifices that can break a young girl's heart. An American skier even gave up her fiancé for the sake of Olympic skiing. In a letter to her sister, the star explained the circumstances: "I have made a painful sacrifice to remain a racer. Last fall I started dating a boy. I fell very much in love with him. I didn't realize it, but my skiing went really bad. Instead of practicing, I spent my time with him. It showed in my speed on the slopes, but who cared? Then I was moved to the Olympic team. I had to choose. I went back to my practice schedule with a vengeance.

"About two weeks ago, I received a phone call from my fiancé. He wanted me to marry him and forget skiing. I told him I was sorry, that I did love him, but that I was going to ski. He wished me all the luck in the world and said good-bye."

To get ahead in the ski racing world, performance is what matters. Fast talkers have no place here because everything is recorded—*time* for Alpine and cross-country events, and *distance* plus *form* for the jumpers. Complainers also meet up with "not wanted" signs. Some time ago, about one hundred ski racers competed against each other at a special training camp. One outstanding young skier told his friends that the coaches did not give him enough attention. His unhappiness showed when the Olympic team was chosen. Although he was a good racer, he was not selected.

For jumping events, there are five judges who have the complicated task of measuring the jumper's achievement. They go by a point system. Points range from 0 to 20, and these are given for the three parts of a ski jump: the take-off, the flight, and the landing. In addition, points are given for distance. At one time, style was not important, and over the years a few people continued to suggest that a jumper be judged only by how far he can leap. But this idea has never been accepted, and it is unlikely that it ever will. Jumping for distance alone would make the sport dangerous. So if you become a ski jumper, you will lose points for wrong body movement in the air, for crossed skis during the flight, for a fall while landing. You may keep your arms in front of you or at your sides, but you must be steady. Spectators like to watch ski jumping best of all. It is a beautiful sight when a man soars off the run and through the air. Jumping seems to require much courage, but proper practice is essential. At the famous jumping school for boys at Winter Park, Colorado, the training starts with tiny jumps and works its way toward the higher jumps. More champions have come from the Scandinavian countries—Sweden, Finland, Norway—and from the rest of Europe, including Russia, Poland and Germany, than from the United States. But lately, with youngsters beginning to jump at an early age, Americans are starting to make a mark in the international jumping world. John Balfanz, one of the best Americans, once pointed out that you don't have to live in the Rocky Mountains

to become a ski jumper. On the contrary, many of the best United States jumpers come from the East and the Midwest. In fact, Michigan is the cradle of American ski jumping.

When jumping is combined with a fifteen-kilometer (9.3 miles) cross-country race, it's called a "Nordic combination." The competitors' results are combined. But if you hear the expression, "special jumping," you will know that the competition is jumping alone, without the cross-country racing.

It is not difficult to learn cross-country skiing. You can try it in a large park, and then join some friends for a longer trip in the hills. The basic cross-country steps are picked up in a few weeks, though it takes years to perfect them. The steps consist mainly of a "glide" and a "kick." You strive to ski with the least effort and to achieve a special rhythm. The equipment weighs little, and the cross-country experts do no huffing and puffing. In fact, to the better Nordic men, the long miles through wintry nature are an excursion. Although in the United States the cross-country skier is just beginning

The biathlon entry must be an expert cross-country skier and marksman.

to be appreciated, in Scandinavia he is a hero. There he is greeted at the finish with laurel wreaths and kisses and parties.

A cross-country skier's physical reserves must be very great. Only the healthiest individuals can become winners. Distances are counted in kilometers; a kilometer—km., for short—is exactly 0.621 of a mile. Could you manage fifty kilometers, or thirty-one miles? Could you go—without a stop—uphill and downhill for thirty kilometers? Could you sweat out a course of even fifteen kilometers? This is what men must do in cross-country competitions. For women skiers, the cross-country is ten kilometers and in some cases only five kilometers. So far, no American girl has had this special kind of ruggedness, but American coaches are trying hard to create male cross-country aces. Most competitive cross-country skiing is done on the university level. College is a somewhat late start for cross-country skiing. A college skier may have been athletic during his high school days but, without the special powers of endurance that Europeans develop when they are

63

Complete concentration is required of all jumpers before shoving off.

Hans Truoel

youngsters, these skiers have a difficult time in cross-country training. The sport is only for very determined people.

So far, the United States Olympic cross-country skiers have not brought home any medals. However, this may well change. In the meantime, this type of competition at least helps create men in America who learn to love the quiet of the forest and the beauty of a winter landscape. And a man who has completed an 18-mile race has been strengthened by it for life.

Cross-country skiing is not a spectator event in most countries. It is really not very dramatic. Although the racers perform real feats of strength, they do nothing visibly sensational. Compared to the downhill racer, they don't go fast. They

seldom fall. There are almost no cross-country injuries, which the crowds always expect in the downhill races. Cross-country skiers wear no crash helmets. They are not as dashing as their Alpine colleagues. Indeed, they are modest and quiet. They are started at thirty-second to one-minute intervals—to disappear, one by one, in the deep forests. Here they struggle for supremacy. Although they use the same narrow trail, the weaker athletes must step aside to let the stronger ones by. Not many spectators wait to see the finish.

Slalom and downhill are another matter, especially in the Alps, where public schools are closed when important races take place. It is a joy to watch a slalom. The course is short, and runs on a steep hill. If you stand midway up the course,

Good form, as well as distance, is prerequisite for winning this race.

you can see the racer at the start. He wiggles his skis back and forth, testing them. You hear the count-down. The racer bursts off the starting platform. If he is good, his movements are swift and smooth. Before your eyes he swings, snakes, dances, weaves through fifty to seventy-five slalom gates. His skis do not scream on the hard snow surface—they whisper. You are witnessing an unforgettable sight.

The gates are made of eight- to nine-foot bamboo poles. On the poles are colored flags. Yellows, reds and blues stand out against the snow. At the bottom, there is a finish marker, and the judges and timers gather around. Along the way, each slalom racer is carefully observed by gatekeepers.

The competitor must go through a tight maze, which seems complicated to the onlooker. Many slalom poles are set in long vertical lines. Sometimes, two bamboo poles stand horizontally. Other gates are combinations of the above. These figures take memory, concentration, skill. A racer must have a refined technique—otherwise, every mistake will show.

A slalom racer tries to go as fast as possible without falling. If he develops too much speed, he may miss a gate altogether. This means disqualification for that race. Even if he wins the second slalom "heat" (there are always two, with differently set flags), his disqualification in the first slalom will halve his chances for a good result.

Speed itself is not difficult to achieve because of the steepness of the slope. With this gravity,

Women skiers stretch automobile inner tubes to strengthen their biceps.

he could go over one hundred miles an hour if he could stand up. But there are the gates, and too much speed might also cause a "spill." After an excellent start, one American champion fell the length of ten gates recently. This meant that he was out of the meet. (He had one run behind him.) Often, a racer tries to get up after a spill and, in good sportsmanship, step through the gate he just missed, and go on again. But climbing even a few yards takes time, and time is most precious in slalom. So a skier cannot retrace more than one gate.

What if two racers finish at, say, sixty-one seconds? How can the timers tell the winner? The answer is simple: On the stopwatches each second is split into ten parts, or ten split sec-

onds. The result of the winner could be 1:1:3, which means 1 minute, 1 second and 3/10 of a second. The next man may just arrive 1/10 of a second later. In the important national and international races, timing is now down to 1/100th of a second. A result may therefore read 53:22. This means 53 seconds and 22/100th of a second.

That is why slalom technique is so important, and why a racer must learn a dozen ways to shave time. This takes superior coaching. A top coach like Willy Schaeffler, whose university teams have won most of the collegiate crowns through the years, can tell each slalom racer exactly what he has done wrong after a run. Schaeffler prepares his competitors early in the fall, and then supervises them constantly during the long winter training sessions, until they are ready for the first races.

What sort of things does Schaeffler look for in a skiing competitor? What kind of advice does he have to give? First of all, he will expect you to ski well. Next, he will impress upon you the importance of memorizing the gate combinations for the slalom. You cannot ski through a combination of three vertical gates by sight alone. By the time you can see them, it is already too late to decide the technique. What you must do is remember the gates beforehand. Good slalom racers are taught to think far ahead.

Competition skiers are all taught the importance of rhythm. They keep their weight far over the middle of their skis because of the steepness of the course. They have learned to keep the use of their steel edges to a minimum. Edges have a braking effect—you already learned this in your snowplow turns—and too much edging robs a competitor of split seconds of time.

Girls make good slalom racers because of their sense of timing and their agility. Slalom speed is less than it is in downhill, where injuries are more frequent and more severe. The giant slalom (which leads down a steep, bumpy, curvy terrain) is faster skiing. There are thirty to fifty widely spaced gates in the giant slalom, some of them wickedly sharp.

To groom a top downhill racer also takes several seasons. It is done in well-planned steps. Coaches gradually increase the length and the steepness of the course, until a skier is able to race down a spectacularly steep slope without fear. The better he gets, the less tired he feels after a long run. And the more speed he musters, the better are his chances of completing the run without falling. In time, he learns the art of recovering balance while plunging downhill at high speeds. Sometimes, barreling around a turn at 60 mph, you find that your legs suddenly are going in different directions. Yet you will be able to bring your skis together again and go on as if nothing had happened. In short, you will fight the falls. Naturally, not even champions succeed every time.

Unlike the slalom racer, who is not allowed to ski through

Junior racer receives helping hand at start of downhill competition.

the flags beforehand, the downhill contestant will study almost every inch of the descent in practice. Then, on the day prior to the downhill, he must take a nonstop run. This is a rule, for it weeds out many of those who do not belong on the course. A nonstop run is like a rehearsal. But it's dead serious. Not long ago, during such a run in a snow storm in Aspen, Colorado, several young racers were injured. One of the young hopefuls, was on crutches for the rest of the season.

What is a downhill start like? Young skiers are gray in the face before the countdown. Their hands tremble and their hearts pound. Veterans control this excitement. They may try a downhill turn or two to warm up their limbs. They force themselves to relax and to concentrate. They take deep breaths. They may even crack a quick joke before a start, but this does not mean they are unaware of what is at stake.

Unless the skier acquires calm nerves, he cannot get ahead in Alpine racing. There are many upsetting moments, but he cannot let them bother him. For example, he could draw a late starting number. This can mean a rutted and more difficult course. Then too, the snow is often different for the first and last starters.

Sometimes purely mechanical things go wrong. In 1965, Billy Kidd turned in a brilliant performance at the Vail Internationals, to which the best Frenchmen and Austrians had also come. Kidd churned down a course with great style and enthusiasm. He had the fastest time that day. Applause greeted him. There was only one problem. The hand-held stopwatches had worked, but the electric timing equipment had *not*. And only the latter was official. His rivals demanded that he repeat the run!

The downhill racer faces weather problems, too. For the forerunner (who always goes ahead of the contestants) and for the first three men, there could be a glaring mountain

But the laurels that await each winner at the finish line are his alone.

sunshine. For racers number four and five, the sun may suddenly disappear behind the clouds. Number six needs extra good nerves. Will his light be flat? Will he see the contours of the steeply falling downhill course? If he can't, he will not know at what point to take a pre-jump. (Pre-jumping is done to clear bumps in a controlled flight—without it, the high downhill speeds might toss the racer into the air.) Now come numbers seven, eight, nine.

The sky is not only cloudy, but a biting wind has started to blow. It is a wind that whips up from the valley, lashing the contestants' faces and hitting their crouched bodies, which downhill racers keep in the so-called egg-position, or tuck. During the same meet, other racers may battle a snow storm, where they see almost nothing through their goggles, and in which they cannot fly—as do pilots in a fog—on instruments. Their only guides are their cool judgment and their ability to learn a course by heart.

On downhill courses, the skier may also face enormous sheets of glare ice. In steep curves, ice is not easy to control unless the contestant has the right skis, and the steel edges have the correct sharpness. Racers ahead may fall. Such falls are often announced over the public address system. How will a contestant feel if he learns that six out of ten downhill racers ahead of him didn't finish the race?

There are other factors that require a cool head. Downhill racing speeds average sixty miles per hour. Seventy and eighty miles per hour are not rare and, under special circumstances, downhill men have gone over 100. At such a pace, the presence of a spectator on the course could be a disaster unless the skier could jump over him.

Downhill training has become much better in the United States than it used to be. For college skiers, it starts in the fall. One of the most rugged programs takes place at the University of Colorado, in Boulder. Here, every afternoon except week ends—which are reserved for glacier skiing—the racers start out with half an hour of rope skipping. Then they dash to the "pits"—a tree-lined, trampled, muddy valley behind the stadium. As Coach Robert Beattie yells, the racers perform the wild gyrations of speed calisthenics. They do countless push-ups, chin-ups, sit-ups, shouting "one, two, three, four" in unison, like Marines. No quarter is given. ("What do you think this is?" the coach rages at a slow nineteen-year-old. "A vacation? Faster, faster! Faster!")

But this is just the start. Under Beattie's stern gaze, the racers have to sprint uphill and down, and do a dozen other exercises. This training lasts several hours, after which they must play football. When the actual skiing starts, many racers feel ready and relieved. To a few, it is even fun.

How do you become a ski competitor? There are several ways. Many young people start through ski clubs. Here, they compete against each other in races that are not "classified" or official. In mountain communities, you can begin racing at an early age — the earlier the better.

There are all sorts of races for fun at ski resorts, which anybody can enter. At one Colorado area, there is a yearly race for hotel and restaurant employees. They go downhill as fast as they can, carrying loaded trays. In Taos, New Mexico, there is a marathon fun race where the competitor skis the same hill as often as possible during the same day. One man has done it sixty times. (He is over fifty years old.) Most ski spas, like Sun Valley, organize races for guests according to sex, age and skill. If you are just a beginner, you should enter these.

Dream fulfilled for three skiers.

Franz Votava, Austria

Racing can be more serious in high school and college. If you make the team, you compete against other schools.

Most of the best American coaching talent is concentrated in colleges, and good ski programs are worked out. Some colleges even offer special scholarships for outstanding skiers. Our Olympic teams are made up, to a great extent, of college racers. This is not the case in Europe.

Most American races are under the authority of an important ski body called the U.S. Ski Association, which has its headquarters at the Broadmoor Hotel, Colorado Springs, Colorado. Here are the locations of the eight divisional offices:

Rocky Mountains: 520 Boston Building, Denver, Colorado.

Alaska: 1111 E. Fifth Avenue, Anchorage, Alaska.

Central: 205 E. Front Street, Traverse City, Michigan.

Far West: 812 Howard Street, San Francisco, California.

Intermountain: Box 17181, Salt Lake City, Utah.

Northern: Box 81, Kalispell, Montana.

Pacific Northwest: Box 434, Yakima, Washington.

Eastern: 98 Main Street Littleton, New Hampshire

In Canada, it is the Canadian Amateur Ski Association.

The U.S. Ski Association has made a giant effort through the years to collect the necessary monies for competition. (Remember that our government—unlike others—does not contribute funds toward the United States international skiing effort.) The USSA also makes sure of safety precautions (which get more strict every year, in the hope of cutting down on accidents), and helps to pass along and enforce the rules established by the world ski body. This is the FIS, standing for the *Federation Internationale de Ski*. (If you want to take a look at the many complicated rules of racing, you can obtain a rule book from the USSA for $2.)

In the U.S. Ski Association offices, you will meet some of the many enthusiastic volunteer workers who make the Alpine and Nordic meets possible—the starters, referees, timekeepers, course-setters and chiefs of course. The USSA and its divisions also publish bulletins, run ski huts, help coaches, establish the ever-larger training camps for racers, and appoint all sorts of committees. To the racer, though, the USSA's most important task concerns his racing credentials. These are called "classification cards."

At first, you are a "novice." Then you become a "C" racer, and get a "C" card from the Association after a certain number of "sanctioned" (official) races. After more meets, which vary in each division, you become a "B" racer and, finally, after still stiffer requirements, you are an "A" racer. Along the way, you receive points which, as they build up, promote you to a higher class.

The teams we send to world championships naturally consist of the elite "A" racers, and it is the dream of every top competitor to represent the United States. Such teams compete against other nations in the Olympic Games, the FIS championships and, in certain years, take part in international races at Wengen, Switzerland ("Lauberhorn race"), and Kitzbuehel, Austria ("Hahnenkamm race"), as well as several others. The winter Olympics of 1968 will be held in Grenoble, France.

Although ski racing itself is no career, it will provide many satisfactions. It will make a skier strong, healthy, and self-confident. But racing does not create wealth.

On the other hand, successful American racers have gone into some phase of the increasingly profitable ski business. With a famous name, a champion is in demand to sell skis for a manufacturer. Some skiers have opened stores or become coaches. They are wanted to manage ski schools and ski areas. They do ski publicity or ski photography or ski writing.

But it's really a long way from the first race to the moment you earn your living in the ski industry—if that's what you may want to do. You'll first have to learn how to ski. Then you will have to train and train and train.

Mathias Zdarsky, Austrian ski pioneer of about one hundred years ago.

Chapter Six

A SHORT HISTORY OF SKIING

Though skiing as a *sport* is new, as a means of getting places it is as old as man. When it started—more than five thousand years ago—a ski was used as a snowshoe, for the Scandinavians had found out quickly that they would sink into the snow unless some contraption held their feet on the surface. The early Norsemen needed to ski to hunt and, of course, for travel. Drawings of old skis were found in Russian caves, and actual skis turned up in Finnish marshes.

A German sports historian, A. C. Luther, claims that some sort of ski, made largely of bone, existed in ancient China and Korea. In fact, some experts say that skis go back ten thousand years. You will find some fine examples of old skis in the ski museums of Oslo, Stockholm, London and Basel, or in the *Ski Hall of Fame* at Ishpeming, Michigan. Some of the skis, we are told, came from the bent planks of early Viking boats. The Vikings quickly discovered that skis could serve as transportation in warfare. We have evidence that skiers took part in battles near Oslo around the year 1200, where it was reported that King Haakon's two-year-old son was carried to safety by men on birch slats.

Three hundred years later, one of the great ski episodes took place in Scandinavia. Did you ever hear of the Vasa Cross-country Race, which is held in Sweden every March? It is the world's longest (eighty-five kilo-

Ski in back, left, points to area where sport originated—Scandinavia.

meters); it involves the most competitors (up to 3,000).

The Vasa race goes back to Gustav Vasa, who made war against the Danes as a revolutionary in the sixteenth century. This was the time when the Danes had sent sheriffs and noblemen to control a part of Sweden. Riding through the countryside on horseback and by wagon to mobilize his fellow countrymen, Gustav came to central Sweden sometime in January, 1521. Here he gathered farmers along his way and asked them to join him in a battle to shake off the foreign yoke. Arriving at Mora—at that time one of numerous small, famine-stricken villages around a lake—Gustav Vasa was disappointed. His efforts appeared to have been in vain. The farmers had not shown much enthusiasm for his project because it was too risky. He determined to leave Sweden before his enemies could catch him.

Gustav Vasa planned an escape into Norway and was soon on his way, skiing toward Salen, close to the border. By now, Gustav's countrymen had changed their minds and decided to give him their support. Legend has it that they called on the two best ski runners in the area to follow Gustav and ask him to come back. The two men caught up with him at Salen and persuaded him to return to Mora, where he successfully raised a large peasant army. Thanks to Vasa, who later became king, the Swedes drove out the Danes and firmly established their self-rule.

Skis were also popular among the Lapps. For stopping, they used a long stick that looked like a broom. Their left ski was much shorter than the right. The lighter ski was employed for gaining speed, much as the left foot can be used for pushing a roller skater today.

Through the ages, all kinds of strangely shaped skis made their appearance. Some looked like narrow canoes. Others were like a mixture of snowshoe and ski.

European hunters of 1870's tracked game on skis, or "Norwegian shoes."

"Neither rain, nor snow . . ." stopped the mailman on his duty in the American West. These hardies of a hundred years ago are delivering mail on skis. A single wooden pole helps them push through the snow.

There were also wooden snow skates. Norse ballads tell us of the old ski god, Ullr, and of a goddess named Skadi who left her husband because he did not want to move to the snow-clad mountains, but preferred the beaches. As for Ullr, you may still find him on good-luck charms that skiers wear.

Skis play an important part in the life of the Norwegian people, too. Without skis, people would be snowbound for several months each winter, but with skis they can attend to all kinds of work that involves moving about. They continue to hunt and shoot on skis after heavy snow has fallen. Some-

times they go to weddings and funerals on skis and, in an emergency, the doctor or the midwife can rely on skis. The farmers are always glad when they hear the distant sound of the post horn and the postman arrives on skis with messages from relatives and friends.

In earlier times, every Scandinavian community and valley developed its own type of ski, and each farm had several pairs. On Sundays, people went to church on skis, and afterward they often skied away from church, down the hill on which the church was traditionally built.

Until the last century, Scandi-

78

navians used a toe strap on their skis and one long stick as a brake when skiing downhill. Most of the skiing for sport rather than utility took place in Telemark and Christiania. Here ski bindings were introduced, and it became possible to jump on skis. Skiers could now go downhill at great speed and even make turns and bends.

"Slalom" was introduced. The expression came from the words "sla" (for slope) and "lom" (for trail). Of course, these old slaloms required no flags, and the Norwegians used the natural terrain—trees and rocks—as the markers. Skiing had now become a world-recognized sport. It soon spread from the North to the Austrian Alps and even the other end of the world—to Australia, where skiing is now immensely popular, and to New Zealand. Men were also skiing in Greenland and Japan, where there are many enthusiasts today. Eskimos, of course, also used skis.

A British ski historian, Howard Bass, tells us that the first military ski race in Norway took place in 1767. The Scandinavians kept displaying their knowledge of handling what they still called "snowshoes." In some countries they were mocked because the skiing idea was still so new. Besides, their graceful turn—which they had named the "telemark" after the Norwegian region where it originated—did not work well in the steep Alps. (In performing the telemark, you advanced one ski and turned your body around it). Some of the Scandinavian skiers fell down on the slopes, to the great merriment of the Swiss and the Austrians. After the Norsemen were gone, the people kept trying the sport themselves, and sought out more gently sloping valleys where they would not be laughed at as they learned to ski.

By the 1850's, many Norwegians had gone to California in search of gold. Other Scandinavian immigrants rattled west in covered wagons over the bumpy trails. A few sailed to the West Coast by ship and moved on the land on foot. Spreading to Oregon, Nevada and Colorado, the Scandinavians soon showed their daring on skis, which many had brought with them.

Before long, the miners began to organize ski races in camps

79

This youngster is trying his luck at jumping on the fine ski slopes at St. Moritz, in Switzerland, just before the turn of the century.

with strange-sounding names like Poker Flats, Onion Valley and Poorman's Creek. We have good records of how these men would assemble in the mountains of Nevada and California. Their skis were four inches wide and up to thirteen feet long—or even longer. For poles, each man had a single stick that was as high as his head. If the starter's watch can be believed, some of the skiers' speeds came to 70 miles per hour. (In 1873, one Sierra skier was even said to have reached 87 mph.) They raced for purses of gold, and for the joys of motion after the long day mining. With money at stake, the races could become rough. Sometimes a greedy miner would try to trip his fellow racer with his pole.

The run itself was 1,000 to 2,-000 feet long, with the finish line most often straight under the start. This meant that the skiers ran close to the fall line, on a slope of 35 degrees, which is as steep as modern downhills. Much later, in other parts of the world, control began to be important. For some races, ashes were even strewn to slow down the runners who came to prefer courses with turns in them. Not so in California. Speed and sheer courage were all that counted. The miners even slicked their wooden boards with secret formulas—mostly tars and candle wax and special oils and beeswax. A few smeared lard or herring under their skis.

An old California newspaper

Skis were vital part of equipment for this Austrian soldier of 1906.

gives a good account of how the rugged men of a hundred-odd years ago went all out in their racing: "There is a breathless silence for several seconds. Suddenly you hear a gun shot. The miners start to stab the snow with their sticks. They pole for dear life and some strike their own skis by mistake. This makes them fall, with great shouts and curses.

"Now they are running 40 miles an hour, now 60, then at the rate of 70. Here one runs over a rough place and loses his balance—his skis fly in the air and touch one another. Away he goes and throws another, and heads, legs, arms, poles and perhaps broken shoes are turning in 20- to 50-foot somersaults, amid a cloud of snow, raised by the current of air produced by their fall and velocity. And if the skis are not broken, they shoot off in the air like an arrow, or like a riderless warhorse in battle, over the snow field, and leap often several feet high in the air, until they run against a tree or into a ravine, where they get stuck on the other side if they do not go again over the next hill in the snow bank." Whoever reached the bottom first—in one piece —was the winner.

One of the most interesting characters to come out of this California period was Jon Torsteinson, a Norwegian who renamed himself "Snowshoe" Thompson. One day in 1856, Thompson heard that the postmaster was looking for a man to deliver the mail to distant mining camps. There was no railway yet, and it seemed that no stagecoach was able to cross the forty-foot Sierra snowdrifts. Mail riders and men on foot had failed, too.

Thompson was a good skier and a man of tremendous physique and stamina. He applied for the job to carry the mails from Carson Valley to Placerville. Soon he was lugging up to

81

A ski pioneer, Hannes Schneider.

fifty pounds of letters and packages ninety miles on skis weighing twenty-five pounds. Without Thompson, many mining camps would have been without candy, tobacco, and newspapers. Soon people began to depend on Thompson to deliver medicines and ore samples, to rescue frozen miners from a cabin, to find lost prospectors, and even to transport a newborn baby in his pack.

There are no secrets concerning Thompson's knowledge of the country. "He reads his bearings in the stars, the trees, the lichens and the moss on the rocks," said one 1859 newspaper account of him. "His compass is the drift of the snows, the flow of streams, the tracks of animals."

In spring, when the Sierra Nevada Mountains turned into a heavy, mushy softness, Thompson would make himself a bed under rocks in the daytime and travel at night by the moon or the light of his lantern when the snow had frozen. Thompson had the route for many bitter winters until the railroad came to replace him. He braved blizzards and sometimes Arctic temperatures that would plum-

met to thirty below zero. He fought for his life with wolves. In the end, he also had to fight with the United States government for part of his post-office wages.

Thompson never got his wages. He was buried a poor man at Genoa, Nevada, in 1876, and his gravestone bears two crossed pairs of skis. "Gone but not forgotten," reads the inscription. In the eyes of Bill Berry of Reno, Nevada, who unearthed parts of his story, the Norwegian is one of the most unforgettable figures of the West—a Kit Carson and Paul Bunyan all rolled into one.

Soon after Thompson's death, the California gold rush came to an end, and the Norwegian skiers went elsewhere. For awhile, jumping took over as a sport—mostly in the Midwest and northern New England,

In the Thirties, America saw a heavy influx of European ski instructors.

Union Pacific Railroad

where special clubs sprang up one by one. In the West, loud Scandinavian bands led the way to jumping hills next to the mines, and one day in 1888 the men gave an exhibition. When you think of an Ole Sunlie or a Lars Jamtaas or an Erick Geswold, you have a good idea of the nationalities of the early American ski jumpers. They were all Scandinavians.

In Norway, similar men with long mustaches built small platforms from which they could leap into the air on skis, landing thirty feet farther down. For a few years, other types of competition were forgotten in Scandinavia and the rest of Europe, and in the United States as well. Jumping took over, lock, stock and barrel staves (which still served many youngsters as skis). Jumping was so popular that 10,000 people turned up near Oslo to watch one competition. The jumpers would hold themselves erect during the flight, their arms going like windmills. Finally, their ski tips would dip and they would come in for their landing. (It was to take skiers until the 1920's to develop the streamlined style of modern jumping.)

Among the early Norwegian jumpers was a man named Fridtjof Nansen, who was to have a profound effect on skiing. In 1888, Nansen set out on a dangerous expedition on skis across the ice fields of Greenland. A few years later— again on skis—he started a long, hard journey he hoped would take him to the North Pole. He wrote a book about his exploits. Translated into many languages, the book was to arouse new interest in skiing.

One of the most important ski pioneers was an Austrian, Mathias Zdarsky. Born in 1856, he began to experiment with skis as a boy. Up to then, most bindings were still made of cane or braided straw. By 1905, the ingenious Zdarsky had put together and tested more than 150 new ideas to lock the foot onto the ski. He also invented a special tent, studied avalanches, and set up the world's first slalom using gates. More important, on the steep mountains above his native village of Lilienfeld, he developed a better maneuver to turn and stop than the Scandinavian "telemark." His skis were much shorter than those we have described, but he

crushed to death by an avalanche.

A truly golden age of skiing had long since begun. In 1904, the United States saw the birth of the National Ski Association (later the USSA). It was composed mostly of Norwegian ski clubs. Soon the Dartmouth Outing Club in Hanover, New Hampshire, and the Lake Placid Club in upper New York State were founded—both to become powerful influences in the sport. In Germany, Willi Paulcke demonstrated the sport to large crowds. In England, Vivian Caulfield wrote the first useful ski-instruction manual in English. In Switzerland, Arnold Lunn—later knighted by Queen Victoria—began to draw more Englishmen into the circle of skiers. Lunn, who had put on his first skis in 1898, was no doubt the great influence on Alpine ski racing. He set up a modern-style slalom in the Swiss town of Muerren on January 6, 1921, and he also introduced modern downhill races, founded the Kandahar race, the Inferno race, and helped to write rules. Gradually, because of Lunn's work, many of the Brit-

Clothing and transportation have been streamlined since the Thirties.

Union Pacific Railroad

87

ish aristocracy caught ski fever.

Much of ski history was also written in a tiny Arlberg village named Stuben, where the Austrian mountains rise as high and steep as angels' wings. You have no doubt heard of the Arlberg School of skiing and of Hannes Schneider, who was among the first to develop it. Schneider completely banished the _____ and finally the stem christ_____ the deep crouch came _____ Schneider taught thousands how to shift their weight when turning. He set up a real ski area at St. Anton, assembled instructors, and adopted steel edges from a man named Lettner. Schneider's pupils and his films carried the message all over the world: Skiing was now possible on the steepest hills and in any kind of snow. And skiing was joy!

So was racing, with the advent of better hickory skis and genuine ski boots. Step by step, racers worked away at technique. Anton Seelos perfected parallel turns. A young, tanned French racer, Emile Allais—one of Seelos' pupils—pushed the improved method to new heights. Dick Durrance, an American student in Bavaria, startled the world with his speedy tempo turns, and his daring on the downhill courses.

Rugged American skiers gathered forces in the eastern United States, bringing the 1932 Winter Olympics to Lake Placid. And they continued to the Rockies, often at dawn, to soar down logging trails, meadows, the paths above Estes Park and Winter Park, Colorado. A crude ski tow opened at Shawbridge, in Canada; another—apparently the first in the United States—was built at Woodstock, Vermont. A historical marker still reminds us of it: "In January, 1934, on this pasture hill of Clinton Gilbert's farm, an endless-rope tow—powered by a model T Ford engine—hauled skiers uphill for the first time. This ingenious contraption launched a new era in winter sports."

In several states, American financiers began to put up money for ski resorts. Men like C. V. Starr and Roland Palmedo got interested in Stowe; Averill Harriman's enthusiasm and the Union Pacific Railroad's money brought about Sun Valley, Idaho, where a banana-company engineer put up the first chair lift. To the Aspen-Ashcroft region came a Swiss expert, Andre Roch. All over the nation, Forest Service recreation specialists laid out trails and began to encourage construction of more lifts and lodges and hotels. In an advertisement for Sun Valley, a skier showed his tanned chest and his glistening face. Discovered: the benefits of sun for skiers!

During the 1930's, foreign ski instructors and coaches truly invaded the United States. It all started with Otto Schniebs ("Skiing is a way of life"). Then came famous people like Sig Buchmayr, Hans Hauser, Otto Lang, Friedl Pfeifer, Walter Prager, Sigi Engl, Sepp Ruschp, Hannes Schroll, and finally the father of modern skiing himself, Hannes Schneider, fresh from the clutches of the Nazis who had imprisoned him. James Laughlin, American publisher and ski enthusiast, still remembers how Schneider stepped off the train and onto his new home ground of North Conway, Vermont, to walk "under the crossed ski poles of the New England villagers."

In those days, United States skiing still had much of an Austrian-Swiss flavor. On the other hand, the National Ski Patrol Service was an all-American achievement. There were small patrols all over the United States before 1938, volunteers faithfully driving up to Mt. Hood, Oregon, in their model T's, or up to wind-blown Berthoud Pass, Colorado, or to then-untracked Mt. Greylock, Vermont. Arriving on week ends over rutted roads, some of the early patrolmen came armed with accident whistles and toboggans made of skis, and primitive, boatlike rescue sleds. Their own hickory skis had droll bindings that opened on the side, or "revolutionary" Kandahar bindings with a front lever that never managed to snap open when the skier fell.

Much of the organization of a national ski patrol network was due to a New York City insurance man, Minot Dole, who had suffered a bad ski accident himself. Dole persuaded enough skiers to join the patrol, asked regional doctors to give their free time, and tapped socialites for funds. First aid supplies were often short, and early patrolmen tore sheets into bandages, or cut up grocery cartons

89

Modern ski troopers in Alaska.

to make splints. Later, the Red Cross helped.

When World War II broke out, Dole's organization already had 1,500 volunteers. The remarkable NSPS founder hurried to the War Department, where he suggested that his men could act as air spotters, wilderness experts, mountain guides and, foremost of all, ski troops. The Army refused his offer. But Dole didn't give up; he literally talked himself through a cordon of officers until he wound up in front of General George C. Marshall, the great U.S. Chief of Staff.

It turned out that the most recently issued U.S. Winter Warfare manual dated from 1914, and the NSPS was indeed needed. Eventually, they were instrumental in recruiting and training the Eighty-seventh Mountain Regiment, which soon grew into the famed Tenth Mountain Division. In all, the NSPS screened and trained over 25,000 soldiers for Uncle Sam's forces. In January, 1942, Dole and an aide, Edward Taylor, stormed an Air Force general's office with a new scheme: the NSPS could help as rescuers in winter.

"We can find stranded pilots by ourselves," the general told them. But Dole insisted that the NSPS' lifesaving ability should be put to a test. If a plane would drop a streamer anywhere on the winter-shrouded Rockies, ski patrolmen would find it within five hours. "Try it!" the general said.

A day later, Ed Taylor and fourteen ski patrolmen waited tensely at a small mountain town while a plane took off from Denver's Lowry Air Base with the streamer. It was dropped on a chilly 12,500-foot peak. The pilot radioed back

Ski patrol, a nationwide volunteer organization, aids skiers in trouble.

the position, which was transmitted by phone to the skiers. Four hours later, they had reached the streamer. Skis still dripping, they raced back to the astonished general.

He quickly agreed that the NSPS knew mountains and snow, and from then on NSPS search and rescue units combed the United States and the Arctic for lost pilots and crews.

World War II proved the importance of skis in many parts of the world. The small nation of Switzerland stood ready on skis to defend its country. The German Army used skis in their campaign against Russia. After parachuting, the British Airforce pilots healed their wounds in the snow fields of Switzerland.

When the war was over, Tenth Mountain Division veterans returned from Italy and went home to every corner of the nation. They injected new spirit, new ideas, and new methods into a dormant ski industry, and started it on the postwar boom that is still going strong.

The impact of ski troop veterans on American skiing is still phenomenal. Their spirit and experience in overcoming physi-

91

cal obstacles led to the development of dozens of ski areas. The exchange of ideas and the experience brought on by the mingling of the nation's best skiers in one unit resulted in new standards of equipment, technique, and facilities for American skiing. A glance at the roster of Tenth Division men still active in the ski industry reads like a Who's Who of the sport.

The late 1940's also saw a revival of ski racing. Americans were getting better: A pig-tailed Gretchen Fraser got us an Olympic First gold medal. Jack Reddish and George Macomber were champions. We began to have some splendid home-grown jumpers like Gordon Wren and Art Devlin. A small band of special ski writers began to make names for themselves. Men like Wolf Lert, Frank Elkins, Alex Katz, Burt Sims, Roland Palmedo, James Laughlin, and David Rowan started to tell the rest of the world about American skiing.

The sport grew in popularity, yet skiers still made up a fairly small family. In the late 1940's "we all knew each other," recalls Frank Elkins. "We were part of a growing but still somewhat intimate activity." Now there were many fast-moving rope tows that often broke down, especially when they had been set up in four or five sections. "The rope virtually catapulted you up the mountain," Elkins remembers. This was the age of ski bums, and of men in baggy pants and windbreakers who explored the still untracked American mountains.

Many old-timers kept scaling America's peaks on foot, skins glued to their skis for upward support, or with their skis shouldered. One Seattle girl has not forgotten the satisfactions of touring: "We could study everything we saw. We knew all the animals and where we could find water. Even the barks and resins of the trees had a special smell." For one reason or another, the fraternity of skiers grew everywhere—the rich as well as the poor.

Then came the 1950's, and with them American girls like Andrea Mead Lawrence, who won us more gold medals; and a brilliant, daring young skier named Buddy Werner, who was to die on skis in a Swiss avalanche disaster in 1964. Among

Werner's adversaries were foreign champions like Anderl Molterer, Stein Eriksen, Christian Pravda and the world's best skier to date, Toni Sailer. Eventually, American girls grew in racing stature. You know the names of Penny Pitou, Betsy Snite and Jean Saubert. And, for the first time, American men— Jim Heuga and Billy Kidd—won medals at the Innsbruck Olympics. From Austria, there had come the wedeln technique, ten years in the making and the result of many racing film studies. Much of this exacting work was done by Dr. S. Kruckenhauser and a small staff who worked in the Arlberg, not far from where Hannes Schneider had first tried his stem christies. In the late 1950's, translations and articles appeared about the new Kruckenhauser method.

Some Americans greeted wedeln with laughter. At a few schools, instructors were even dropped because they taught it. But other ski professionals had open enough minds to pick up the ease and elegance of the short swing. Among them was Willy Schaeffler, who brought the idea to the attention of *Sports Illustrated* Magazine, which helped sell the new method. Different names were used, but when the instructors got together for a yearly meeting most of them already skied in the same fashion. Now there is a unified system of ski-school instruction. It is called "The American Technique," and several American ski school directors deserve the credit for it. Among them are Doug Pfeiffer, Curt Chase, Bill Lash and Willy Schaeffler, who helped with this book. When our skiers recently demonstrated the technique at an international ski congress, there were words of praise even from the sophisticated Austrians who started it all.

The U.S. Ski Association now has eight divisions instead of seven. There are 1,200 ski clubs all over the nation and perhaps as many as 5,000,000 American skiers. There are more and more ski areas. At present, you can ski in thirty-five of our fifty states, and some day you may ski in every state.

Every day, another youngster grows up to discover the wondrous beauty of a snowflake and the glittering snow field that begs descent on skis.

GLOSSARY

ALPINE—Developed in the Alps. Alpine competitions include slalom, giant slalom and downhill.

ANGULATION—At an angle leaning *away* from the hill. See COMMA POSITION.

BINDING—The metal contraption which holds the boot to the ski. Most bindings now come with automatic releases.

BREAKABLE CRUST—A frozen snow surface, with soft snow underneath. Tricky for the beginner who does best by traversing if the slope is steep, or going straight if it is gentle.

CAMBER—The amount of curve under the ski between tip and tail.

COMMA POSITION—The skier looks like a comma, with shoulders leaning away from the slope, and knees and hips into the slope. The same as ANGULATION.

CORN SNOW—Spring snow. Can be grainy or wet, but especially pleasant to ski before the noon sun turns it into a heavy mass.

COUNTER-ROTATION— When the upper body moves in the direction opposite the ski tips. Rotating means turning around an axis.

DOWNHILL SKI—The ski which is farthest downhill and nearest the valley. See also UPHILL SKI.

EDGES—The useful metal strips under skis. *Edging* is the employment of the edges.

EGG BEATER—A slang word referring to a high-speed fall, head over heels.

EGG POSITION or *tuck*—A crouching, deep-down stance for the downhill descent or race. It lowers wind resistance, thus increasing speed. Takes a lot of practice and strength.

FALL LINE—Let a ball roll downhill. Its straightest, steepest, most direct course is the fall line.

GIANT SLALOM—A longer slalom than the usual run, but with wider and fewer gates. The result is a controlled downhill.

HERRINGBONE—A method of climbing a hill by scissoring upward. The skier's tracks will look like so many "V's," or like fishbones.

KICK TURN—A way of changing direction from a standing position, both on steep slope and on the level.

NORDIC—The competitions developed in the Nordic, or Scandinavian countries. They are still favored there: cross-country racing, jumping and biathlon (ski and shoot).

NOVICE—Beginner. Also called a snow bunny.

NSPS—National Ski Patrol System. A unique organization made up of some professional patrols and an even greater number of unpaid volunteers. Their major purpose: To make the slopes safe for skiing and to save the injured skier.

POWDER SNOW—Light, unpacked snow—the newer, the better.

PARALLEL CHRISTIE—A fast turn during which skier keeps his skis together. This is the basis for the short swing.

PISTE—The French word for a downhill run. Mostly, a track over packed snow.

ROTATION—An old-fashioned system of using the shoulders to achieve a turn. The upper body is used like a steering wheel.

SCHUSS—Comes from the German word, *shot*, and means shooting downhill without a turn.

SCHUSS BOOMER—A ruthless downhill runner, who might go "Boom!" into someone else.

SITZMARK—German for the imprint left by those who sit down in the snow. The hole you make when you fall.

SLALOM—A fast, skill-demanding ski competition through fifty to seventy-five gates. Also an excellent way for noncompetitive skiers to improve their ability to make turns.

SNOW BUNNY—A beginner.

SNOWPLOW—Literally plowing the snow. Your almost-together ski tips form a "V." Handy way for a beginner to slow down and stop.

SPILL—A fall. Even an expert takes one, once in awhile.

STEM TURN—A turn accomplished from the traverse by weight-shifting, parting of ski tails and then bringing them together again. A stem christie is the same—only faster.

TRAVERSE or TRAVERSING—To cross the slope on skis. The downhill ski must always bear the major share of the weight.

UPHILL SKI—Crossing a slope, the upper ski is the uphill ski, the one farthest from the valley.

USSA—U.S. Ski Association. Composed of clubs and individuals, the USSA develops and watches over U.S. competitors; it also helps and advises recreational skiers.

VORLAGE—From the German, meaning *forward lean* (pronounced: fore-lah-guh). The weight of the body sits well over the balls of the skier's feet. In general, the steeper the slope, the more *vorlage* is required.

WARPING—Bending, stretching and contracting of a ski when it gets old.

WEDELN—Word comes from German and means "wagging" (such as a dog's tail). A number of fast, rhythmic, snakelike downhill short swings—all linked. Can be done on steep slopes.

BOOKS ON SKIING

There are many other books about skiing. The author likes the following best of all:

Bowen, Ezra. *The Book of American Skiing.* Lippincott, 1963. A banquet of U.S. ski history, with descriptions of ski personalities, ski areas, ski fashions. Mr. Bowen had access to the photo files of *Sports Illustrated* and *Life* magazines, and he enhances his sparkling text with hundreds of photos—some of them in color.

Bradley, Miller & Merrill. *Expert Skiing.* Grosset & Dunlap, 1963. Three ski experts put their heads together to create the first complete ski book for the advanced skier. Details about Nordic jumping and cross-country skiing are presented with clarity. A book for the ski mountaineer, too.

Casewit, Curtis W. *Ski Racing: Advice by the Experts.* Arco, 1963. The first and so far only book devoted exclusively to ski competition. Racing, jumping and cross-country techniques were gathered from many top competitors on both sides of the Atlantic. The book includes 200 dramatic pictures, many anecdotes, tips, and the records.

Day, Frank. *If You Can Walk, You Can Ski.* Crowell-Collier, 1962. Simple and clear, for the average, nonathletic beginner. Many instructors claim that you can't learn to ski from a book. You can from this one!

Estin, Peter. *Skiing the American Way.* John Day, 1963. Again, a modern approach to language as well as skiing. In a terse, easy-to-understand style, the late Peter Estin takes you from the first hesitant steps on the level to wedeln down the fall line.

Hutter, Clemens. *Wedeln: The Austrian Technique.* Doubleday, 1960. The American technique grew out of the Austrian one, with some slight changes. Hutter was on the spot when Dr. Kruckenhauser created his ski revolution, and he knows whereof he speaks. His sequence photos are hard to find elsewhere.

Liebers, Arthur. *Complete Book of Winter Sports.* Coward-McCann, 1964. Here is an idea which, to my knowledge, has not been done so well before: a total summing-up of and introduction to all the winter sports, from skiing to skating to lesser known snow activities. A unique book for the flatlander who wants to keep healthy in winter.

O'Rear, Johnny and Franker. *Skiing Illustrated.* Barnes, 1956. An old and rare book written for children under the age of twelve. The authors have done a fine job of bringing this sometimes complicated sport to a level that can be understood by the young. Many photos.

Pfeiffer, Doug. *Skiing With Pfeiffer.* Pfeiffer Books, Box 1411, Denver, Colorado, 80214. Third printing, 1962. One of America's most experienced ski instructors and ski writers, Doug Pfeiffer has written a complete, well-illustrated course in skiing. His witty book ends with ski specialties such as propeller hops, gazelle christies, the gelaendesprung, the umsprung and the quersprung.

Professional Ski Instructors of America: *The Official American Ski Technique.* PSIA c/o USSA, 1964. This is the ski bible for experts, would-be experts and those who want to become ski instructors. All the ski figures of the new American technique, as well as ski theory, ski mechanics and ski physics are explained in necessarily technical language. Material on avalanches and a history of ski instruction are included.

Schaeffler, Willy and Ezra Bowen. *Sports Illustrated Book of Skiing.* Lippincott, 1960. The man who had much to do with the introduction of the new ski technique in America and the former ski editor of *Sports Illustrated* magazine teamed with America's best sports illustrator, Robert Riger. Result: one of the most popular advanced ski books of all time. Includes pre-season exercises.

Ski & Ski Life magazines, *Ski Pointers by the Experts.* In hardcover: Harper & Bros., 1961. Or in paperback: Award Books, 1964. The cream of America's ski instructors—McCullouch, Engen, Johnston, Engl, Bourdon, Valar and others—give easy-to-understand tips on all phases of ski technique, ski equipment, and ski care.

95

THE AUTHOR AND HIS BOOK

Curtis Casewit was born in Germany, and educated in Italy and France. He holds a degree from the International Language Institute of Florence, and he used his linguistic training as a translator for the British 5th Army during World War II. He came to the United States in 1948 and settled in Colorado.

Mr. Casewit's writing career began with magazines; later he was a staff reporter for the *Overseas Weekly*. Since then, he has written fantasy, adventure, true crime articles, and science fiction for adult readers, as well as teen-age fiction. He has won fiction and mystery magazine awards, and has received praise for his work as translator for the Alpine division of the U.S. Olympics Committee.

Mr. Casewit's articles have appeared in more than fifty magazines, and his best-selling book, *Ski Racing: Advice by the Experts,* is a standard work.

SKI FEVER (Hawthorn, 1965) was designed by Laszlo Matulay and completely manufactured by Western Printing and Lithographing Co. The body type is Caledonia; display type, Venus Medium, Bank Script.